STORMS!

Tales of Extreme Weather Events in Minnesota

By Martin Keller and Sheri O'Meara

the *Minnesota* series

Welcome to the Minnesota Series

S *torms!* is the first in a collection of books titled The Minnesota Series. In addition to *Storms!*, in coming months you'll read about Minnesota music and sports legends, famous crimes, newsmakers, media, politics and more. Each book will be informative and filled with photos, and we hope a memorable and enjoyable read. We will gather stories both above and below the radar, reminding and informing our readers about Minnesota events, personalities and history. These are books that will remind you of what we were doing when. Books will be available statewide where books and magazines are sold or at minnesotaseries.com. We invite you to enjoy the first and following editions of The Minnesota Series!

Authors **Martin Keller, Sheri O'Meara**
Foreword **Belinda Jensen**
Meteorology Consultant **Frank Watson**
Editor **Sheri O'Meara**
Web Consultant **Risdall Advertising, New Brighton, Minn.**
Printing **Bang Printing, Brainerd, Minn.**
Broadcast Weather Radio **KTLK 100.3 FM Twin Cities**
Travel Consultant **Sun Country Airlines**
Publishing and Production Management **Jim Bindas, Books & Projects LLC**
Publishers **D Media: Debra Gustafson Decker, Dale Decker**

©2006 by D Media Inc., 4601 Excelsior Blvd #301., Minneapolis, Minn. 55416.
(952) 926-3950 dmedia@juno.com. www.minnesotaseries.com.
Subscriptions Available at www.minnesotaseries.com
Frank Watson can be reached at watsonwx@aol.com, through his website at
WeathermanWatson.com, or by phone at (651) 762-2774.

ISBN 0-9787956-0-1 978-0-9787956-0-3

Library of Congress Control Number 2006932364

Contents

Foreword

I think it is clear I have Meteorological Affected Disorder, or "MAD," as my good friend climatologist Mark Seeley calls it. In fact, he discovered the disorder, and he has it, too.

I noticed the symptoms early on. I found myself as a young kid wondering what could make the air so chilly in the morning when I had to jump in the St. Croix for swimming lessons every summer. I always cherished the beautiful, toasty autumn days with the beautiful peak colors probably a little earlier than the regular kid. I even remember when my high school physics teacher, Mr. Gavin, used clouds to describe a physics theory; that was the one thing I remembered and liked about that class.

So it makes sense that I end up in this career of forecasting the weather every day. As frustrating as that can be here in Minnesota, I love it and I wouldn't give it up for anything! Part of the lore of Minnesota weather are the events in *Storms!* — the first book in The Minnesota Series. Making our way through the four seasons at this latitude is what makes our weather such a big part of our lives. Enjoy reading about these amazing weather events. If you remember all of these, then watch out: You might have MAD, too!

Belinda Jensen, *Chief Meteorologist, KARE 11 TV, Minneapolis-St. Paul*

The Armistice Day Blizzard
Nov. 11, 1940

In an era when cell phones, Internet and television keep us
in the know around the clock, it's difficult for modern-day
Minnesotans to appreciate the isolation and devastation of one
of the deadliest blizzards in state history: The Armistice Day
Storm. But ask older Minnesotans where they were on Nov. 11,
1940, and they'll recount the experience as if it were yesterday.

On Nov. 6, 1940, there was much to talk about. Newspapers proclaimed results of the Presidential elections the day
before, when Franklin D. Roosevelt defeated Wendall Wilkie,
putting FDR in office for his third term. At coffee shops and
watering holes throughout the state, Minnesotans debated and
planned for the United State's looming involvement in the war
in Europe. But in Minnesota just one week later, all talk turned
to weather.

The Armistice Day Blizzard ranks second on the
Minnesota State Climatology Office's top five weather events
of the 20th century. Only the 1930s dust bowl outranks it.
The storm struck without warning on Nov. 11, 1940. By the
time it was over Nov. 12, the blizzard had killed 49 people in
Minnesota and more than 150 nationwide — burning in
Minnesota's collective memory a warning of the intensity of
winter's wrath.

On the morning of Nov. 11, temperatures topped
60 degrees in many areas of Minnesota. Flowers were still
in bloom. It was an unusually warm fall, the kind of Indian

(photo: Minnesota Historical Society)

Summer that gave procrastinating homeowners reason to put off, for just one more day, installing the storm windows or stocking the woodpile. Duck hunters statewide took advantage of the mild holiday.

Armistice Day — now Veteran's Day, which marks the end of Word War, I — was a holiday for many Twin Cities schools. But not elsewhere. A Brooklyn Center man, 7 years old on the day in 1940, remembers the morning in his one-room country school in Cordova in Southern Minnesota: "It was warm in the morning, with kids in shirt sleeves and many people without coats and boots. The sun was shining. No one knew what was coming."

Indeed, weather reports gave no indication of the massive storm brewing. The early-morning Twin Cities forecasts for Nov. 11 called only for colder temperatures and a few flurries. In the Armistice Day Storm book *All Hell Broke Loose*, Bob De Haven, who in 1940 was program director at WTCN Radio, recalls: "Storm warnings were broadcast as they were obtained from the U.S. Weather Bureau in those days. They were inadequate and not intense or extensive."

But there were inklings. The very few who were watching the barometric pressure that day knew something bad, something unprecedented, was on its way. As the morning wore on, the weather changed rapidly. The sky turned black, temperatures dropped, and rain began to fall. The rain turned to sleet, then to blinding snow ("snowflakes the size of nickels," according to one eyewitness), which began coming down at the rate of 3 to 4 inches per hour. Then came winds that one newspaper report later described as "the winds of hell."

Mild weather ahead of an intense low-pressure system tracking from Kansas to western Wisconsin was quickly followed by a raging blizzard. Many people were caught off-guard by the severity of the storm and the plunging temperatures. Women were caught in the uniform of the day — dresses. Few people had coats. No one had boots. Sixty-degree temperatures the morning of Nov. 11 were followed by single-digit readings by the morning of Nov. 12. In Collegeville, students at St. John's University struggled through 27 inches of snow. In the Twin Cities, 16 inches of snow brought travel to a halt. Winds of 50 to 80 miles per hour created 20-foot drifts.

All told, the storm cut a 1,000-mile-wide path through the middle of the country. On Lake Michigan and Lake Erie, six shipwrecks claimed 66 lives. The Witches of November had struck again.

By noon Nov. 11 in Cordova, the snow was bad. A farmer with sled and team showed up at the one-room school and took the kids to neighboring houses to wait out the storm, wherever there was room. There they stayed for three days, families split up with no way to know where anyone else was.

Telephone and telegraph lines went down, cutting off communications and plunging rural areas in particular into isolation. Those who had working radios clung to them for news — the listeners of KWLM in Willmar no doubt thanking God for broadcaster Harry Linder, who started the town's first radio station that year. In St. Paul and Minneapolis, when travelers reached safety at a place of business or in the home of a stranger, many would send word of their whereabouts to WCCO Radio. For three days, Cedric Adams kept busy at his microphone, announcing on air the location of loved ones, separated from their families tuned in at home.

In the Twin Cities, the blizzard paralyzed transportation, with nearly 40 street cars off their tracks in Minneapolis due to ice buildup, and cars blocking streets — all of which sent hundreds of commuters to the few downtown hotels seeking shelter, taking every available room (sometimes a dozen to a room, according to some news reports) and bunking down for the night in lobbies and restaurants. In New Brighton, nearly 100 people were stranded following a 30-car accident on Highway 8. In Meeker County, poor visibility caused a Soo Line train to crash and collide with a freight train.

Duck hunters, primarily on the Mississippi River, accounted for the majority of fatalities in the storm, many hunters trapped in remote stretches along the river when the blizzard hit. It is estimated that 30 duck hunters in Minnesota and Wisconsin died in the storm.

The Forest Lake Times describes the sight above the wetlands that day:

"The hunters that afternoon saw a sight that was almost unbelievable. It was unforgettable. The ducks, with their instinct of seeking shelter in a storm, flew in, in droves. They came in over the trees and dipped down low. They were coming from all directions and flying at four or five different levels against the fierce wind and snow. The hunters saw big green-headed mallards hover in the air with their wings spread, actually flying backwards. They chose the biggest and best ducks, of course. It was a thrill of a hunter's lifetime."

In their excitement, many hunters did not heed the

warning overhead. Outdoorsman Babe Winkelman holds up
Armistice Day 1940 as a warning of the dangers of hunting.
In a magazine column, Winkelman writes of the day:

"Heavy rains changed to sleet, which morphed into
snow. As many as 20 inches fell throughout the river system.
Visibility was next to zero. Barns and buildings were flattened.
Iced-over power lines snapped. Motorized traffic came to a
standstill. Still, shotguns barked throughout the Mississippi
River backwaters. The hunting was so good that many hunters
couldn't bring themselves to leave for shore.

"While many hunters finally got off the river, many
tried to brave the blizzard in their makeshift blinds. Many were
marooned on islands throughout the bottomlands and froze to
death. Still others tried to get off the river, but waves capsized
their ice-riddled skiffs."

Still, the day yielded hundreds of heroic stories, with
Minnesotans helping one another survive. Out on a river, one
duck hunter recalls finally reaching shore in the blinding snow
and driving winds, only to be stopped by the sound of three
gunshots, which he recognized as a signal of distress. He made
his way back to the river through the storm and searched and
located two hunters, nearly dead, clothes frozen to their backs.
He was able to get the pair off the lake to safety.

Throughout the state, strangers opened their homes
to strangers, sharing their homes and their meals for days.
There were moments of camaraderie amid the tragedy. Travelers stranded at the Minneapolis Greyhound bus depot for the
night were treated to a burlesque show, when the marooned
performers at the Gaiety burlesque theater directly across the

street invited them over for a free performance. The makeshift audience made its way across the street by forming a human chain through driving wind and hip-deep snow.

A few Minnesotans got lost in their own farmyards in the blizzard and froze to death. Others persevered. At one Southern Minnesota farm, only one boy in his family of nine made it home to wait out the storm alone. He was able to get the livestock in the barn, and making his way back to the house in the blinding snow, he bumped into something. Realizing it was the mailbox, far past the house where he was headed, he dropped to the ground and felt his way along the edge of the driveway, and by touch, made his way back to his door.

By 4 a.m. Nov. 12, it was 5 degrees in Minneapolis. Twin Cities newspapers that morning began reporting storm fatalities including death by exhaustion, freezing and car accidents. It would be three days before many families were reunited. But in the aftermath of the storm, Minnesotans got busy. A pilot flew over Lake Pepin, dropping whiskey and food to surviving stranded hunters. As the death toll mounted, families mourned, and churches buried their loved ones. With school canceled, entrepreneurial boys joined a crew of 200 who spent days shoveling out Memorial Stadium, to prepare for the University of Minnesota's remaining football games of the season (a priority, since the Gophers were No. 1 in the nation that year).

Out in the country, farmers counted their losses, and were disappointed, still coming out of the Depression, to find it would be a lean Thanksgiving that year. Half the turkey crop in Minnesota, Wisconsin, Nebraska and Iowa had been lost to the blizzard. In Minnesota, the Martin County Historical Society reported that 9,400 turkeys were lost. *The Forest Lake Times* reported that the Thurnbeck farm lost 2,000 of their flock. In Stacy, one family lost 9,000 turkeys between two farms. On the Peterson farm in Chaska, with many birds frozen solid, women canned 200 jars of breasts and thighs in 2-quart jars, according to the book *All Hell Broke Loose*. "The next morning one old turkey gobbler was spotted strutting around, and Mr. Peterson butchered him," recalls Peterson neighbor Benjamin Anderson in the book. "He weighed 27 pounds dressed. He was then sent to the governor as a gift."

In the weeks following the storm, U.S. Weather Bureau was taken to task for failing to predict the state's biggest blizzard in history. Correspondent Mark Steil discusses the events in a story for Minnesota Public Ratio:

"Officials knew a storm was coming but were wrong about its strength and scope. But perhaps the most embarrassing revelation was that no one was watching the storm's explosive development in the predawn hours of Nov. 11. A retired government forecaster says the Midwest headquarters in Chicago was not staffed overnight. The uproar led to several changes. The Chicago office went to round-the-clock operation and the Twin Cities branch was upgraded so it could issue forecasts."

On Thanksgiving Day 1940 — while Gov. Harold Stassen dined on Mr. Peterson's turkey and began formulating ideas how to change Minnesota weather reporting — other Minnesotans no doubt bowed their heads and said an extra prayer of thanks for making it through the storm. Sixty-six years later, Minnesotans have endured other blizzards, and other storms are now more top of mind. But no blizzard has claimed more lives than the storm of Nov. 11, 1940. The generation that lived through the Armistice Day Storm still has stories to tell.

Selby Lake Streetcars backed up in the wake of the Nov. II blizzard.
(photo: Pioneer Press)

Cars stuck in snow, Armistice Day Blizzard.
(photo: Minneapolis Star Journal, Minnesota Historical Society)

With Gopher games yet to play, workers clear snow out of Memorial Stadium following the blizzard. (photo: Minneapolis Star-Journal, Minnesota Historical Society)

Cars on and off the road, Armistice Day Blizzard.
(photo: Minnesota Historical Society)

A truck stuck in the snow following the Armistice Day
Blizzard, Minneapolis. (photo: Minnesota Historical Society)

Digging out from the blizzard.
(photo: Robert Keagle, Minnesota Historical Society)

Governor Karl Rolvaag (in Minnesota Twins cap) inspecting the 1965 flood damage.
(photo: Guy Gillette, Minnesota Historical Society)

The Great Floods
April 1965

The official letter from Minnesota Gov. Karl F. Rolvaag to the president of the United States, Lyndon Baines Johnson (LBJ), had the quiet intensity that underlies all levels of government when disaster strikes, people are in need and property is threatened. Readers of this story will be reminded of the desperation and debacles of the Gulf Coast with Hurricanes Rita and Katrina in August 2005. But in spring of 1965, there were almost as many dire situations in southern Minnesota and the Twin Cities, all related to high water. Rolvaag wrote:

"I...do urgently request that you declare a major disaster, encompassing the political subdivisions listed below, and that you authorize Federal aid in the connection therewith, in accordance with the provisions of Public Law 875, 81st Congress."

The date was April 18, 1965. Floodwaters along every major river system in Minnesota were reaching dramatic levels, breaking historical crests, washing away homes and businesses and causing the evacuation of thousands of people from Mankato to Rochester and Hastings, including the Twin Cities. But it was not limited to Minnesota. Flooding damaged areas in the entire upper Mississippi and North River Basins, including parts of eastern North Dakota in the Red River Valley, western Wisconsin, northern Iowa and down into Illinois and Missouri.

The Midwest spring usually comes with a sigh of relief

in these parts — especially if the winter has been rough and snow-heavy. But a big dog called "fear" often chases it. As the seasons moved from the long winter of 1964–'65 to the welcomed spring solstice, it seemed a whole pack of mad dogs had been turned loose, especially on the cities of Mankato and Winona. On April 10, the Minnesota River peaked at a record-breaking 29.07 feet in Mankato, according to the commemorative Picture Story publication that same month from Mankato Graphic Arts and Advertising Unlimited Inc., titled "Last Great Flood?". A record crest at Winona of 20.8 feet in 1965 was reported in a retrospective story about the Great Flood in the *Star Tribune* May 1, 2001, when high excess water was again an issue in the Twin Cities area.

Mankato, which bore the brunt of the flooding, had seen other great floods in 1952 and 1871. But in 1965, revisionists went to work, rewriting the history out of necessity and explaining how it happened. The preceding fall, a deep frost of 11 inches put more than the usual amount of water into Minnesota's rich soil. The frost served as a fuse that was later lit when a rapid — but late — thaw took place a few months later. A blizzard near Mankato on March 18 brought "the accumulated snowfall" to 59.6 inches, the "Last Great Flood" account states.

The water content of the snow alone in the area between St. Cloud and Mankato equaled 9 inches. But then the dogs piled on. Extensive rains on April 4 and 5 added to the rapid runoff of fast-melting snow, ground thaw and escalating ice jams. The calamities always associated with spring flooding ensued — only this time at the top of the scale. You couldn't blame nature; it was just doing its job. There was simply the cumulative effect of too much water everywhere. The massive spring flow surged through rivers, creeks and streams to their natural watershed point, the Mississippi, where it drained to the Gulf of Mexico, just like the system still does today. But on land, the natural cycle prompted mass evacuations, rigorous sandbagging and the arrival of the National Guard — and eventually, money from Washington.

On April 29, in a "rush" telegram to Rolvaag, LBJ released $3 million dollars "to effect the assist authorized in my declaration of 'A Major Disaster' in your state on April 18, 1965." By then, much of damage had already been done to the infrastructure as Rolvaag's plea of April 18 outlined, including "highways, bridges, culverts, roadbeds, and storm and sanitary sewer systems."

In places like downtown St. Paul, where the Mississippi rose to 26.01 feet, according to the *Star Tribune* of May 1, 2003, Kellogg Boulevard was transformed into a canal alongside the mighty Mississippi. On April 8 the river stage in St. Paul was 5.6 feet. It crested at 26 feet on April 16.

Using flood forecasts, St. Paul citizens and city government officials added plywood extensions on top of its floodwall five days before the river would crest. But some places weren't fortified enough: The walls of the historic Minnesota Boat Club on Raspberry Island in St. Paul were washed away by the ravaging waters, reported *Meetings: The Journal of Minnesota Hospitality*. The facility had been there since 1870. Meanwhile, out in Stillwater, inmates freed temporarily of their prison walls were used to construct emergency dikes along the St. Croix

River, the National Weather Service reported.

In Minneapolis on April 18, the legendary Stone Arch Bridge, just off downtown, was still active with trains rolling over its rail bed that sat atop the same big river. "Suddenly and without warning…Pier 7 of the bridge settled uniformly about 14 inches" — with a train sitting on it! Rapidly advancing water moving at an estimated velocity of 13 to 14 feet per second during the flood's peak caused it to sag, according to the "Report of Damage to the Great Northern Railway Company's Stone Arch Bridge" from the U.S. Army Corps of Engineers District, St. Paul. Several stones from the arch fell into the river as the moving water scoured out the sandstone base of the arch's footing to a depth of more than 14 inches.

Along the gorgeous 22 miles of Minnehaha Creek, from its headwaters at Lake Minnetonka down through Edina, Hopkins, St. Louis Park and south Minneapolis, flooding was also a major issue. People built dikes around their homes and got out of water's way. But nature was not the only culprit in this great flood: Intense development along the creek and other areas prior to 1965, which included the draining of thousands of natural wetlands that help prevent against floods, only added to the troubles. Millions of feet of hard-paved surfaces — roads, driveways sidewalks, gutters and curbs, and huge parking lots — flushed and forced more water into the watershed rather than allowing it to be absorbed where it fell as precipitation or melted snow. Those same man-made conditions still prevail today, including the extensive use of drain tiles on farmlands that add to our collective water-management issues.

In the aftermath of the Great Flood of 1965, a few

outstanding statistics tell the rest of the story:

→ **More than a million sandbags were used in North Mankato alone, according to the Mankato Picture Story publication.**

→ **The flood caused $103,200,000 in damage to public and private property, reported the U.S. Army Corps of Engineers.**

→ **In Mankato and North Mankato, 1,500 families evacuated. Estimated damage was $5 million.**

→ **In St. Paul, 200 families evacuated their homes. Estimated structural damage: $700,000 (1965 dollars).**

→ **The *St. Paul Pioneer Press* reported a total of 22,000 Minnesotans were driven from their homes.**

→ **Fifteen deaths were attributed to the floods (U.S. Army Corps).**

→ **The Red Cross reported that 21,000 people suffered losses during the episode.**

→ **Agricultural damages were significant, including the disruption of the planting season (U.S. Army Corps).**

→ **The Star Tribune of June 25, 1993, recounted how the 1965 floodwater came within 18 inches of reaching the transformers at Black Dog Generating Plant for Northern States Power Co. in Burnsville, the largest plant of its kind at that time.**

→ **The National Weather Service tagged the rampaging water as the greatest flood in more than 100 years along the upper Mississippi River for a distance of nearly 700 miles.**

The Minnesota legislature in 1955 established the Minnesota Watershed District Act to help manage water resources and to educate about erosion, flooding and other issues tied to land uses and waterways. But many districts did not become reality until after the Great Floods of 1965. In

1967, the Minnehaha Creek Watershed District was founded, the second-largest watershed in the state covering 181 square miles and including 29 cities, including portions of Minneapolis, Edina, Hopkins, St. Louis Park and many other towns.

Still, no matter how hard humans try to manage their natural environment, it's nature that ultimately governs. Less than a month after the great '65 flood, five major tornado funnels were sighted in the Twin Cities area on May 6, causing widespread damage. The U.S. Army Corps of Engineers report of June 30, 1965, indicated that, "30 separate touchdowns were recorded."

Teenagers building a dike, Stillwater.
(photo: Minnesota Historical Society)

Kellogg Boulevard looking east during flood, St. Paul.
(photo: Minnesota Historical Society)

Embassy restaurant during flood, Burnsville.
(photo: Minnesota Historical Society)

View of St. Paul showing the flood's devastation.
(photo: Philip C. Dittes, Minnesota Historical Society)

When major Minnesota events were being broadcast in the early days in the
Twin Cities, Stuart A. Lindman was on the job. Lindman was the first person ever to
appear on what is now KARE-11. He signed WMIN-TV on the air for the first time in 1953, serving
as newscaster, news director and program director. He continued as news
anchor then director of public affairs after the station merged with WTCN-TV in 1956,
then later changed its call letters to WUSA and still later to KARE.
(photo: courtesy of Pavek Museum of Broadcasting)

One of Minnesota's best-known weathermen, WCCO-TV's Bud Kraehling sometimes worked from the "Shell Weather Tower," an elaborate set at the time with weather maps, dials and gauges. (photo: courtesy of Pavek Museum of Broadcasting)

The Edmund Fitzgerald Storm
Nov. 10, 1975

The legend lives on from the Chippewa on down
Of the big lake they call Gitche Gumee.
Superior, they said, never gives up her dead
When the gales of November come early!
— *Gordon Lightfoot. "The Wreck of the Edmund Fitzgerald"*

The morning the big ship loaded more than 26,000 tons of
taconite pellets inside the harbor of Superior, Wis., the
weather was reportedly calm and lightly overcast. It was Nov. 9,
1975. Indian summer in the preceding days had graced "up
North" with warm temperatures, blue skies and a false sense
that the coming winter season had been cheated one more day.
The tourists who had come for the fall colors were long gone.
But a few lingered along Duluth's Canal Park in its pre-devel-
opment days. It still looked like an industrial tract of land
covered in warehouses along the lakeshore. There were next
to no restaurants on Canal, or the flashy hotels like today. A
couple kids plugged two bits into binoculars and trained them
on the distance as an ore carrier prepared to depart the
Superior port exit to the south.

It was early afternoon by the time the 29-member crew
of the 17-year-old SS Edmund Fitzgerald, once the largest ore-
carrying steamer on the Great Lakes, set off for Detroit. There
in Motown its cargo would be blasted into steel for manufactur-
ing cars, and the big boat would travel finally to another port

Members of a U.S. Coast Guard Board of Inquiry, in white coveralls, inspect
liferings and other debris of the sunken ore carrier S.S. Edmund Fitzgerald in Cleveland,
Ohio, Nov. 23, 1975. (photo: AP)

where it would be shedded for the winter. Meanwhile, two weather systems hundreds of mile apart had already embarked for an unforgivable rendezvous on the big water with the hardworking men and their historic ship.

Few storms live in the public memory and abide in the cultural lifeblood of Minnesotans like the Nov. 10, 1975, hurricane-strength force that framed the sinking of the Edmund Fitzgerald on legendary Lake Superior. How and why she sank is still debated today even after the official inquiries had listed all known details and tried to answer the questions still asked years later. The bodies of its crew members have never been found. Could four of the hatches that less than two weeks earlier were documented as damaged contribute to widespread flooding in the cargo hold? Did the Fitz strike the dangerous Six Fathom Shoal and wreck its hull up near Caribou Island before she disappeared forever?

Was it also hit by something in the water, causing it eventually to break in two and crash into the murky silent depths 600-plus feet below? Did its seasoned captain not know how mortally wounded she really was? Or was the Fitzgerald simply overloaded with taconite after its legal loading limits had been increased three times and was simply unable to withstand the intense 90-mile-per-hour wind gusts, pounding 12- to-25-foot waves and, later, the blinding snow? Perhaps it was a combination of all these factors — and others that remain unknown.

Gordon Lightfoot's brilliant retelling of the ship's fate in his international pop hit a year after the horrible event can still cast a chill and mist an eye even 30-some years later with its ancient poetic meter and haunting melody sung in a rich, seafaring baritone. The tragedy also inspired documentary films, news stories, books, and even a 1986 play, "Ten November," staged at the Actors Theater of St. Paul by a host of its finest musicians and playwright Steven Dietz, storyteller Kevin Kling and songwriter and lyricist Eric Peltoniemi. It was produced again for the 30th anniversary in 2005 as a musical titled "The Gales of November," this time — appropriately enough — at the Fitzgerald Theater in St. Paul. But it's still Lightfoot's "The Wreck of the Edmund Fitzgerald" that immediately captures nearly every aspect of the storm.

The song grew right out of the bedrock of North America's storied folk music traditions, imported from the British Isles and grafted with numerous regional influences from the Southern Appalachian Mountains to the Canadian Maritimes. But at the heart of the song that fervently eulogizes the ship and its crew lies the matter-of-fact dread produced by the forces of wind, water, air pressure and something else ultimately unknown that conspired to turn a routine commercial voyage into an unforgettable shipping disaster and human tragedy.

Lake Superior's history is as vast as its 31,700 square miles, and it is cursed and blessed with its own weather system. So awesome in size, this largest freshwater body in the world has often been called the sixth ocean. Its maritime stories could fill several volumes of books: Its shipping and trading lineage alone extends back before the earliest explorers set foot on the lake shore where the Anishinabe (or the Ojibwe or Chippewa) had already learned to respect the coldest and deepest of the Great Lakes. In time, Superior's many visitors, captains and sailors were forced by the lake's many moods, weather patterns and quiet deceptions to pay it the same respect.

> *That good ship and true was a bone to be chewed*
> *When the gales of November came early.*

The Fitz steamed out into open waters, with Master Ernest McSorely at the helm. It was warm and the skies had cleared. A nearby companion steamer, the Arthur M. Anderson, piloted by Captain Jesse "Bernie" Cooper and also loaded with taconite pellets, headed from Two Harbors, Minn., to Gary, Ind., and tailed the Fitzgerald throughout the dark events that unfolded over the next 28 to 32 hours. Both men knew the weather forecast called for "a typical November storm" and stuck to the easterly shipping lanes on the water many called Ol' Treacherous, perhaps one of the most dangerous water environments in the world with its killing cold temperatures and unpredictable nature. What the two captains may have not realized were the distant conditions that eventually fueled this superstorm on Superior, natural forces that would launch them into the news headlines and the history books.

The day before, on Nov. 8, a low-pressure weather system over Colorado — sucking warm moisture from the Gulf of Mexico — started moving Northeast; while up in Alberta, Canada, a similar low-pressure front, this one funneled with numbing arctic air, began its trek eastward across the northern region of the United States.

"The National Weather Service kept a close watch on this system, concerned about what might happen if it slammed into the system moving up from the southwest," writes Michael Schumacher in the preface of his book, *Mighty Fitz*, just one of many fine tomes written about the lost ship. "There really wasn't much room for speculation. History dictated the forecast: in the vernacular, if the two systems met, all hell was going to break loose."

> *The wind in the wires made a tattle-tale sound*
> *And a wave broke over the railing*
> *And every man knew, as the captain did too,*
> *T'was the witch of November come stealin'.*

By nightfall, around 7 p.m. on the ninth, the Weather Service issued gale warnings for all of the lake. By 2 in the morning of Nov. 10, the ship's captain swung her out of the shipping lane and drove the boat northeast, approximately halfway between Isle Royale and the Keweenaw Peninsula. The Anderson, still quite a few miles behind her and in constant touch by radio, followed. According to Frederick Stonehouse's essential account of the ship's final run, also called *The Wreck of the Edmund Fitzgerald*, the captain's strategy followed the old tradition of steam navigation in taking the "fall north route," which offered more protection from northern storms, even though the southern route was shorter although "more exposed and dangerous in a gale."

That critical navigation decision might have cost the lives of its crew and the ship as the winds and waves increased in intensity on their final day. Captain Dudley Paquette, another captain on the lake in the SS Wilfred Sykes, candidly recalled in his book *The Night the Fitz Went Down*, that the original weather forecast — plus errors in understanding Superior's weather history — were mostly to blame for the disaster. Not only did the Weather Service fail in predicting the storm's right track in the foreboding waters of the beastly lake, whose wrath had been riled by the two invading storm centers from the north and south, but the two captains hadn't done their meteorological homework.

"…anyone who knows weather would know they'd be trapped down there as the rotation of the storm system brought the wind around to the southeast, then the east and northeast," Paquette explains. "By the time they realized it was a monster storm, all they could do was turn north and try for lee, an area sheltered from wind and waves, on the Canadian shore. By then, that route exposed them to the worst of the storm on every leg of the voyage – the worst of the northeaster, then the worst of the northwest seas when the wind came around from the northwest."

But was Paquette's assessment too harsh? There hadn't been a storm-related ship lost on Superior since May of '53, when the Henry Steinbrenner succumbed to 70-mile-per-hour winds and 25-foot seas that ripped off her hatches 12 miles south of Isle Royale with 17 men aboard, all of whom perished. While the other Great Lakes had claimed more lives, few professionally sailed onto the Gitche Gumee without the knowledge that despite its majestic sweep that linked three states and one province across two countries, it also was a graveyard for more than 350 ships, an indifferent liquid world where roiling danger zones always lurked, from its deepest fathoms to its

most pristinely forested shorelines far up Minnesota's beautiful
north shore into Canada.

> *When suppertime came, the old cook came on deck sayin'.*
> *Fellas, it's too rough to feed ya.*
> *At seven p.m. a main hatchway caved in, he said*
> *Fellas, it's been good t'know ya*
> *The captain wired in he had water comin' in*
> *And the good ship and crew was in peril.*
> *And later that night when his lights went outta sight*
> *Came the wreck of the Edmund Fitzgerald.*

On the afternoon of Nov. 10, the National Weather
Service noted a significant wind shift at 2:45 p.m. to the northwest at 42 knots, with the Anderson reporting waves of up to 12
and 16 feet. The northwest wind, as Paquette predicted, would
increase the danger to both ships by exposing them to bigger
waves. Now neither boat could be protected by land. Meanwhile, conditions were breaking down across the region: The
storm's fury closed the Sault Ste. Marie locks.

By 3:30 in the afternoon Nov. 10, with the light quickly
fading in the late autumn skies wracked by twisting wind and
endless water, the ore boat was in serious trouble. McSorely
called Cooper and reported that his ship was listing (leaning to
its side). Its fence rail was gone, its radars were out, there was
damage to some vents and two of the pumps were pumping
water but not nearly fast enough to keep up. The ship was
losing buoyancy. McSorely said he would try to make it to
Whitefish Bay, just about an hour away. But now a blizzard of

snow also pelted the Fitz, and the Anderson eventually lost its visual track of her.

In Dr. Joseph MacInnis' compelling account, *Fitzgerald's Storm*, Cooper reported gusts up to 100 miles per hour that afternoon. He said two ghostly waves "30 to 35 feet high" plundered the deck of his own ship around 6:30 in the evening. Worry about McSorely's situation slowly started to set in as the tortured expanse of Superior — and the drama of the two ships — became immersed now in the total chaos of darkness and the fury of the gale.

At around 7:10 p.m.., the Fitzgerald and the Anderson talked again, the Anderson to relay to the stricken vessel that another boat lay up ahead. After determining its postion, the Anderson assured the broken ore carrier that the other ship would not be an obstacle. When asked, "...how are you making out with your problem?" the reply came from the Fitzgerald, "We're holding our own." Then at some point shorty after the poignant exchange between two lifelong sailors and those final words, the lake quickly and violently claimed the Edmund Fitzgerlad. It broke her in two as the forces of water, steel and destiny aligned in the depths of the nightmarish lake.

The story of the ship and the science behind the storm refuses to die. As recently as May 2006, the Bulletin of the American Meteorological Society released a new report based on computer modeling done on the storm, the wind, the waves and the hapless freighter. According to a *Chicago Tribune* story about the report of May 21, 2006, "[storms of this type] ... are seen only once or twice in a decade on Superior, weather scientists found. Worse, the winds blew from a direction that sent them unobstructed over 180 miles of open lake, pushing waves the size of apartment blocks right in the ship's path. The models show the worst of the weather was confined to a small corner of the lake and lasted only a few hours. Into that brief, destructive window sailed the Fitzgerald."

In more poetic language, the Canadian folksinger framed the tragic saga with these heartbreaking lines:

> *And all that remains is the faces and the names*
> *Of the wives and the sons and the daughters.*
> *Lake Huron rolls, Superior sings*
> *In the rooms of her ice-water mansion*

But the lake itself replied almost instantly that night with its own kind of closure and twisted, poetic justice. As if to seek a redemption over all those who traverse this unlikely ocean for whatever reason, or to re-establish its might over those who chart its depths, harvest its resources, scrounge for its treasures and attempt to plot its unfathomable weather, the lake momentarily cleared in the wake of the sinking ship. The snow briefly stopped and visibility was restored. The wind lessened. And Superior's frigid waves once again marked time on the black canvas of darkness and loss, waiting for the dawn.

The largest and longest vessel ever built on the Great Lakes, the 729-foot ore carrier SS Edmund Fitzgerald, slides into the launching basin, on June 7, 1958, in Detroit, Michigan. Two more months of interior work remain, before the $8,000,000 ship is put into service. Her capacity will be 26,000 tons and her speed up to 16 miles per hour. (photo: AP)

Wind gusts up to 45 miles per hour push Lake Superior waves breaking at about 16 feet over the Canal Park pier in Duluth, Minn. A storm like this was the undoing of the Edmund Fitzgerald. (photo: AP)

This underwater photo of the sunken SS Edmund Fitzgerald was taken by an unmanned submersible robot, as a research team investigates the wreck site 17 miles northwest of Whitefish Point, Mich., on August 24, 1989. The 729-foot ore freighter sunk on November 10, 1975, during a severe storm, taking its load of iron and the crew of 29 men to the bottom of the Lake Superior. (photo: AP)

Same storm, two ships, two different fates. One folklore, one still sails. The Arthur M. Anderson ore carrier takes on a load of taconite Oct. 25, 2005 in Duluth, Minn. The Anderson was called upon to help search for the ill-fated Edmund Fitzgerald in rough Lake Superior waters in 1975. (photo: AP)

This is an undated file photo of the Edmund Fitzgerald, which plunged to the bottom of Lake Superior in 1975. (photo: AP)

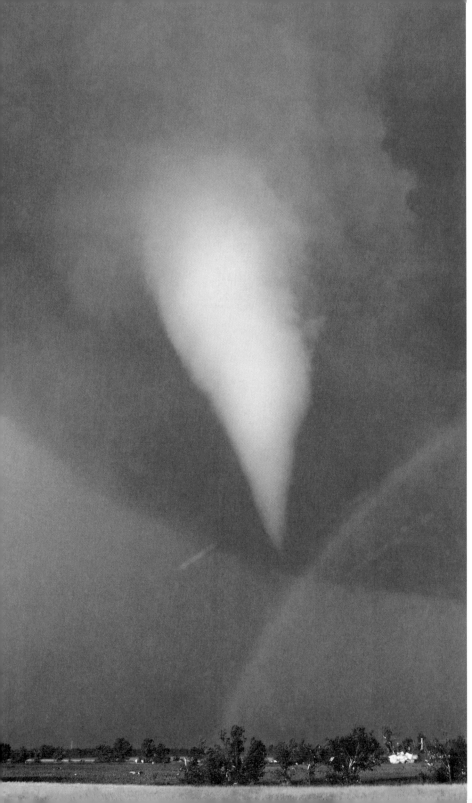

The Television Tornado
July 18, 1986

Not much work was getting done at the small Minneapolis publishing company the afternoon of July 18, 1986. It was the hottest day of the year. The outdoor temperature was 95 degrees, and inside the old brick building, floor fans were of little help, simply moving around the stale, muggy air. Employees were lethargic. By late afternoon, they were also preoccupied, looking out the window at the thunderstorm in progress and talking on the phone, trying to salvage plans for the summer evening. It would be a rainy night at Sommerfest on Nicollet Mall if this continued.

At 4:50 p.m., the excitement level inside the building rose considerably for the employees lingering at work.

"Hey, look at this! There's a tornado on TV."

Staffers gathered in and around the art director's small cubicle, and for about a half hour, they watched a unique drama unfold on a small black-and-white TV, as a tornado skipped through Brooklyn Park, Fridley, Spring Lake Park, Arden Hills and Coon Rapids. KARE-11 helicopter pilot Max Messmer was the man of the hour, as he and cameraman Tom Empey became part of the story they were covering with their rare video of a tornado in action.

Messmer, a former Vietnam pilot, and Empey were already in the air en route to another story when they got word about a tornado in the northern suburbs. It was an F2, and it moved slowly (no faster than 10 to 15 miles per hour, according to reports, about one-third the speed of most tornadoes), allowing the cameras to capture images that would later be studied by scientists to better understand the qualities of the tornado.

For the first 15 minutes, the KARE team provided the only visual account of the tornado, discussing events live on air with anchor Paul Magers. A WCCO-TV helicopter arrived on the scene in time to film the last half of the event, and at that point, both television stations had live coverage of the tornado.

Observers say the KARE helicopter was smack in the middle of the action. On the ground in Brooklyn Park, homeowner Michael McDaniels told the *Minneapolis Star Tribune* what he saw:

"He (Messmer) was far enough away from the funnel cloud to be safe, but when the debris started flying around, I decided he must be nuts," McDaniels said. "Those main rotor blades were taking a real beating and if they went, he'd be in trouble. That close, I'd have been a little scared — it was amazing to watch him."

The filming of the event was a victory for KARE-11, earning the station national attention. KARE had been running a distant third in news ratings, but the tornado put the station's newscast on the map. Empey was using a new device on his camera, a gyro, which helped him zoom into the tornado without the video jumping around. KARE stayed on air without going to commercial for its entire 5 p.m. newscast and went past its 5:30 ending time into the Nightly News time slot. From flying into the tornado, Messmer was nicknamed "Mad Max" after the Mel Gibson character.

But even without the news video, the slow-moving

twister was a sight people stopped to watch that July day.

From *Star Tribune*: "Further away, on westbound I-94, hundreds of rush-hour drivers stopped on the highway as one of the funnels lingered several miles dead ahead, appearing at times to be moving southward down the median. Some got out of their cars to take pictures, others scrambled for shelter under bridges. Overpasses on I-94 and I-694 were crowded with people trying to get better looks."

There may have been an estimated three tornadoes, originating near 85th Avenue and Noble in Brooklyn Park, according to the National Weather Service. But the main tornado that people saw was on the ground for 33 minutes.

There were no deaths and there was relatively little damage for a tornado of that duration. The worst damage was at Springbrook Nature Center in Fridley. The tornado spent more than 10 minutes in the nature center, uprooting 5,000 to 10,000 trees, including thousands that were a century old. Damage there was estimated as high as $250,000. Portions of the park damage were left to help teach about the destructive power of tornadoes. Total property damage from the storm was estimated at $650,000.

Fridley and neighboring suburbs were no strangers to tornadoes. Twin Citians still talk about the three Fridley tornadoes of May 1965, which devastated the area. (The 1965 Fridley tornadoes were among six tornadoes that hit the metro area that day. In all, 13 people were killed and 683 injured in the outbreak.)

So, is it coincidence that a tornado would return to Fridley?

Not if you believe in "tornado alleys," the areas where a tornado is likeliest to touch down according to statistics.

State Climatologist Earl Kuehnast identified the Twin Cities area's two tornado alleys in 1970 — a main alley in the northern suburbs and a secondary one south of the Minnesota River. Five years afterward, he found that more than 85 percent of the metro-area tornadoes between 1959 and 1972 were found in those alleys, according to *Star Tribune*.

There are several theories why the alleys exist — humidity from the Minnesota River Valley, the topography of the northern suburbs, the dome of heat concentrated over the core cities on hot days, deterring thunderstorms in the cities and diverting heat to the suburbs.

No matter the theory, "it's well-established that the alleys are there — no question," meteorologist Bruce Watson told *Star Tribune*.

City officials in Fridley are perhaps not as quick to comment.

Men of the hour: KARE-11 helicopter pilot Max Messmer and cameraman Tom Empey
became part of the story they were covering with their rare video of a tornado in action.
(photo: KARE-11)

The Rain Superstorm
July 23–24, 1987

It's too bad the Weatherball was no longer positioned to display weather warnings in 1987. The Minneapolis weather icon had been removed five years earlier when fire destroyed its home atop the Northwestern National Bank building downtown. If it were still active July 23, 1987, it would surely be flashing nonstop that day, according to the old weatherball jingle:

> "If colors blink by night or day,
> precipitation's on the way."

Was it ever. On July 23 and 24, 1987, the Twin Cities area was hit by the area's heaviest rain ever in 24 hours. Up to 11 inches fell between 7 p.m. July 23 and 1 a.m. July 24, causing the area's worst-ever flash flood. With rain falling as heavy as 2 to 3 inches per hour (combined with another severe thunderstorm 72 hours earlier, which had dumped 4 to 9 inches of rain over the same area), the ground became saturated quickly. The streets filled with water, and roads flooded. Cars floated. Rivers overflowed their banks. Storm sewers spouted. Tornadoes and straight-line winds of 70 miles per hour added to the night. Two men died in storm-related deaths.

In downtown Minneapolis, there were perhaps a few more revelers that night, as happy hour-goers lingered … then lingered some more … then finally holed up in their favorite ports in the storm until nearly closing time. It's a good thing the Minnesota Twins were on the road to their first World

Canoeists paddled east-bound down 494 in Bloomington after the superstorm of July 1987. (photo: Pioneer Press)

Championship away that night, playing the Toronto Blue Jays at the old Exhibition Stadium. Had they played at the Metrodome, some foolhardy fans would've no doubt insisted on leaving the Dome in the deluge, creating an even more impossible mess on downtown streets, which were flooding in the heavy rains.

The storm had the audacity to infiltrate the weather office at KARE-11, with water pouring in and staffers scrambling to cover the equipment with plastic. Minneapolis-St. Paul International Airport was closed for six hours. Portions of the highway system were closed for days. But still, commuters were on the road. According to the *Minneapolis Star Tribune*:

"Drivers found the rain so hard and wind-driven that at times it appeared to come sideways instead of down. It blew through the seals of car windows, and the fastest windshield wipers were no match. ... People swam from their cars in waist-deep water. The State Patrol said the rainstorm closed more stretches of Twin Cities highways than any blizzard had."

Two men drowned in the storm — one in his car and one in his collapsed basement. Shoppers and stranded commuters sought safety in Southdale. "... but water from the parking lot spurted across the J.C. Penney's sales floor," according to a *Star Tribune* story.

The newspaper also reported that, with an official rainfall high of 11.32 inches, there were greater unofficial amounts, including 16 inches near the intersection of highways 35W and 494. "You won't see 10 inches (of rain) more than once in your lifetime in this area," Jim Zandlo, Minnesota state climatologist, told the paper.

It's ironic that the third week of July every year is when Twin Citians celebrate water (albeit area lakes and rivers, not downpours) with the annual Minneapolis Aquatennial festival. But in the weeks following the 1987 festival, as the people of Sleepy Eye honored one of their own (Sandra Polesky, Miss Sleepy Eye) for being crowned Aquatennial Queen of the Lakes—residents of Hennepin and Ramsey counties got busy repairing damage.

"The rainstorm of the century" … "the granddaddy of thunderstorms" … "the superstorm of 87." There were many nicknames given to the storm in the days and weeks following July 23. Whatever the moniker, all agree it hit hard. In Maple Grove, a tornado destroyed at least six homes and damaged some 300 others. Basements flooded throughout the metro area. Roofs and foundations collapsed.

According to the Red Cross, which provided the full range of Red Cross services that July due to tornadoes and flooding, 85 homes were destroyed and 1,977 were damaged. According to the *Minnesota Weather Almanac*, more than $21 million in damage was done to 8,643 residences and 264 commercial properties, with $6 million in damage to public properties.

Oddly, the flooding came in the midst of a drought, which started in October 1986 and lasted through the summer of 1988. Despite the July 23 storm and the one two days earlier, the drought lingered. "The speed of the rainfall and the fact that so much fell on paved surfaces meant that little soaked into the parched earth," a *Star Tribune* story explained.

More bad news came when Twin Citians learned that most water damage to their homes would not be covered by insurance.

But there was a silver lining. The National Weather Service and local media earned high praise for their efforts. It became clear that weather forecasting, warning and reporting on a storm in progress had dramatically improved from days gone by.

"The toll could have been worse, and would have been had prompt warnings not been issued and widely distributed," according to a *Minneapolis Star Tribune* commentary published two days after the event. "The timely efforts of the National Weather Service, the civil-defense system and the area's radio and television stations to spread the word, to identify specific problem areas and to advise area residents to avoid dangerous situations undoubtedly helped prevent further damage injuries and loss of life. Even So, Twin Citians will probably will remember the hard night of July 23, 1987, long after they've forgotten the gentle winter it paid for."

Pedestrians and a lucky dog navigated high water at 90th and France in Bloomington.
(photo: Pioneer Press)

Water stalled cars on University and Transfer Road in St. Paul.
(photo: Pioneer Press)

A Bloomington resident rowed past a garage near Rich Road and Toledo Curve in Bloomington. (photo: Pioneer Press)

The Halloween Blizzard
Oct. 31, 1991

The young couple living in Uptown in south Minneapolis started making their plans the night before Halloween. She would rent the movies tomorrow (spooky films only); he would buy the candy (heavy on chocolate, the better to eat all the leftovers). He would also have to pick up the house. At least the living room where trick or treaters — and their parents — could peer into their rented duplex and see what a frightful mess it really was.

Under a gray sky with temps playing around freezing, she rose that Thursday morning at seven on Oct. 31, 1991, and headed to work while the boyfriend eventually took his seat to telecommute from his computer, just off the small sunroom from the bedroom. A crinkled Homer Hanky lay on his desk. Soon pellets of sleet flecked the windows, a bit of rain and then snow.

She called him at around eleven that morning.

"Can you believe it, it's snowing?!" He could believe it. Hey, this was Minnesota. Weather always played tricks, in every season. He looked out at the piles of leaves on the lawn and shrugged. He was still having a hard time believing the Twins had won another thrilling World Series against the Atlanta Braves, just four days earlier in seven games, the last one going 10 innings. The baseball-frenzied region was still trying to get a hold of itself and get back to normal. Before the storm hit, highs were almost as lofty as those that baseball had induced:

The St. Paul Cathedral in a blanket of snow from The Halloween Blizzard, Nov. 1, 1991. (photo: Pioneer Press)

On Oct. 28 and 29 temps climbed to 63 and 65 respectively. By early afternoon on Oct. 31, the grainy sleet-like moisture and occasional rain from earlier morphed into all snow and continued and continued and continued. And continued.

"Can you believe it's still snowing?!" he asked her by phone in the late afternoon. She told him that she spent her lunch break at the video store and also did him a favor, buying four bags of assorted mini-chocolate candy bars. The roads were getting bad, she told him, icy as heck. He snorted in resignation: Winter was giving everyone a way early preview of its coming attractions. She promised — depending on the roads — to be home by 5:30 p.m., "before the goblins come." She rented the original *Nosferatu* (an ancient movie in black and white); *Don't Look Back* (a Roman Polanski film with Julie Christie and Donald Sutherland, creepy enough for Halloween); and *Young Frankenstein*. The guy didn't think that one was quite right: "It's a comedy."

By the time the five o'clock news shows were on, newscasters were apoplectic with weather angst. This time it was justified. Things were a mess! And, yep, the roads were getting really *bad*! The freezing rain that laid down a bed of ice got layered with heavy snow, which people then drove over. Subsequently it was layered again when the temps plummeted and froze the snow-slush combo on the roads, only to have more snow fall on top of that. And a lot more flakes were on the way as the system was setting up to stall over the area.

Adding to mounting transportation woes as things progressed, MnDOT road crews had been caught totally off guard. Hardly any plows in the metro region had been fitted with blades that early in the season. Plus the storm had come on so soon that ice-melting chemicals had not been put down on the asphalt, either, except for in Ramsey County. Cities were in the same fix: Most were still sweeping leaves off streets when the big one hit. The frozen leaves, thickly compacted with snow, soon wreaked havoc with snow blowers and their operators. Back on the highways the next night at the height of storm, even the big orange plows were getting stuck, or pulled off their routes. The snow was too much for them.

It was a classic Minnesota weather ruse: Fall had secretly donned winter's costume for Halloween as things truly turned ghostly on Oct. 31, 1991, and the day after. Cars disappeared — either buried under drifts — or into garages and driveways, free from streets swollen with the white stuff. People *en masse* just vanished as the reports of cancelled events escalated almost as quickly as the snow depths. By 11 the following night, there was 27 inches on the ground, according to the *Star Tribune*, and nobody was going anywhere: "Metropolitan Transit Commission buses were pulled off the streets at 8 last night, the first time that had happened in a decade. Minneapolis-St. Paul International Airport was forced to shut down for a time late last night."

The storm was really a one-two-three-day event that had its dramatic peaks and formidable details, just like the three-act structure of a good horror flick. First, the foreshadowing of sleet and rain changing to snow. Second, the blinding assault of more snow and wind throughout Nov. 1. Third, the concluding act and numbing resolution of below zero weather (-3) and punishing windchills into Nov. 3 and 4 (as bad as -50 in outstate Minnesota), the earliest below-zero readings ever in Minnesota weather history. When it was all over, weather records were sliced and diced like carved up jack o' lanterns. In the Twin Cities, 28.4 inches fell; in Duluth, 36.9 inches . The National Weather Service reported that at least 20 people had died from car accidents or snow-shoveling heart attacks and other sobering stats. Lots of records fell, including:

→ **Biggest Twin Cities storm: 28.4 inches (Oct. 31–Nov. 3, 1991).**
  Old record: 20.0 inches (Jan. 22–23, 1982)

→ **Deepest Twin Cities 24-hour snowfall: 21.0 inches**
  (Oct. 31–Nov. 1, 1991). Old record: 18.5 inches (Jan. 23, 1982).

→ **Most snow in Twin Cities on Oct. 31: 8.2 inches (1991).**
  Old record: 0.4 inches (1954).

→ **Most snow in Twin Cities on Nov. 1: 18.5 inches (1991).**
  Old record: 3.6 inches (1941).

→ **Earliest autumn below-zero low: 1991 -3 degrees (Nov. 4, 1991).**
  Old record: -1 degrees (Nov. 11, 1986).

→ **Most snow in Twin Cities in October: 8.2 inches (1991).**
  Old record: 5.5 inches (1905).

Further into southern Minnesota and Iowa, an ice storm in the same period with one to three inches of ice, mixed with heavy snows at times, paralyzed that region, closing interstates and stranding hundreds. It was a doosey, alright. In Iowa, Interstate 35 was closed down by fallen power lines: 80,000 homes were without power and there was $63 million in utility damage. Up to 15 percent of the corn crop was still in the fields, and the combination of ice, snow and wind from this storm flattened some fields. Crop damage was estimated up to

$5 million, the costliest ice storm in Iowa history. It took over a week to restore power in some rural areas. Gov. Terry Branstad declared 52 of 99 counties as disaster areas.

In south central and southeast Minnesota, 11 counties were declared federal disaster areas because of the ice storm. The total damage was $11.7 million. According to the National Weather Service publication *Storm Data*, "at least 20,000 people experienced power outages from Oct. 31st to Nov. 2nd, and as many power lines and poles snapped under the weight of the ice. Many rural areas were without power for about a week. Gov. Arne H. Carlson declared a state of emergency in Freeborn and Mower counties. The National Guard was called upon to help provide generators to rural farmsteads while the National Guard armory and a local mall in Albert Lea were both used as shelter for many stranded motorists Nov. 1st and 2nd. At the height of the storm, a 180-mile-long stretch of interstate 90 from South Dakota border to Rochester was closed." It was not a festive trick-or-treat slide into November.

The south Minneapolis couple settled in for the snowiest Halloween either one could remember, and built a fire. They watched outside as the storm dumped its white payload more than they did the film in the VCR, *Young Frankenstein*, the choice of the old Mel Brook's comedy made to lift their spirits, knowing that this early arrival of winter probably signaled a long one, something they both knew too well. By the time the 10 o'clock news came on, not a single trick or treater had gladdened their door. Not one. Now that was scary! They hardly noticed a small weather-related story from back East during a newscast dominated by crazy weather.

According to the National Oceanic and Atmospheric Administration, "an enormous extratropical low" along the entire Eastern Atlantic seaboard in the same period collided when a huge high-pressure system built over southeast Canada, bringing cold, dry air that merged with the low front on the Atlantic Ocean. Called "Nor'easters" in the Atlantic states, this storm was also abetted by the remnants of Hurricane Grace. CNN reported waves of 100-feet or more. "Circumstances alone could have created a strong storm, but then, like throwing gasoline on a fire," the NOAA reported, the fading stages of Grace delivered unfathomable tropical energy to create what the National Weather Service would call "the perfect storm."

While the Halloween Blizzard held forth in the nation's upper Midwest, the Nor'easter storm — what many experts believe was really an unnamed hurricane — sank the swordfishing boat the Andrea Gail and its six-man crew on Oct. 28, on the eastern side of the country. That story produced a best-selling novel *The Perfect Storm* by Sebastian Junger and later a movie of the same name.

What caused Minnesota's white-out at a time when most people are still clearing their gutters, bundling leaves, riding their bikes and enjoying fresh apple cider and doing other fun things and chores before winter? That old haunted combination of warm moist air from the Gulf of Mexico teaming up with a massive cold air front from Canada. When these big acts go on the road together, the result can often be the freakish behavior of the mysterious natural force we call weather, and it can rock our world.

How does it happen? No one seems to know for sure.

But well-known Twin Cities meteorologist Bruce Watson of the National Weather Service told the *Star Tribune* on Jan. 5, 2000, that the Halloween Blizzard could have been caused by "Bruckner Cycles," after the 19th century Swiss meteorologist Edward Bruckner. The cycles, which can overlap, reflect the changes in surface temperatures of land masses and the oceans, the amount of ice on the earth, and changes in solar radiation." Watson identified the Oct. 31, 1991 event as part of the area's Ice Storm Regime (1989–1999).

Perhaps the scariest part of that Halloween storm was its wicked aftermath. Even after the roads finally got plowed, they were in horrible shape and remained so in some places until spring, especially on side streets of well traveled-neighborhoods like those in south Minneapolis. A freaky mid-month November warm spell melted some of the snow cover, when the temp hit 49 on Nov. 13, with balmy highs in the 40's from Nov. 17–21. But it wasn't over so fast.

The Twin Cities got another six inches of snow on Nov. 23 and more than a foot six days later on Nov. 29 — for a 46.9 total inches that month in 1991. Still, many remember the aftereffects of the Halloween blizzard almost more clearly than the storm itself. Even a month later as turkey time rolled around, some roads were still tough to navigate.

"It's like driving on the ribcage of a colossal Yeti!" the guy said, popping another piece of leftover Halloween candy in his mouth as he drove his girlfriend to pick up flowers for Thanksgiving dinner at her mother's. She watched him in disbelief as he unraveled another one and almost lost control of the wheel on the souvenir bumps that the storms had left.

"I can't hear you," she said over the rattle of his old car on the badly rutted street.

"Wha-aa-at did you say?" he shouted.

"I said, 'Stop eating all that candy!' "

Twin Cities streets became "paths" after the blizzard.
(photo: Pioneer Press)

A skier navigates between Twin Cities pedestrians during the snowstorm of 1991.
(photo: Pioneer Press)

A woman walks near the capitol in St. Paul.
(photo: Pioneer Press)

Motorists near Afton pushed through wind gusts of 50 mph.
(photo: Pioneer Press)

On March 29, 1998, 14 tornadoes hit Southern Minnesota, one of the earliest such storms
ever recorded. Churches and Gustavus Adolphus College fell victim to the storm's wrath.
(photo: courtesy of Eric Foss)

The St. Peter Tornado
March 29, 1998

Late in the afternoon of March 29, 1998, almost at supper-time, a service inside The Church of St. Peter had just concluded 30 minutes before the trouble, read the *Pioneer Press* newspaper account two days after the wrath of violent March weather descended on the region. But you didn't need a news-paper if you were in central-southern Minnesota to know how bad the trouble really was. All you had to do was look around at the devastation.

The Church of St. Peter was a Catholic church designed like one of Europe's gothic cathedrals. The city of St. Peter featured an abundance of similar historic properties, from elegant Victorian homes to many other brick-built buildings like the Nicollet Hotel from the 1870s. The Minnesota Histori-cal Society listed 270 such sites for the small town of 10,000, which was originally intended to be the state's capitol.

Over on the tree-lined college campus of Gustavus Adolphus, a few kids were finishing up their weekend activities that same March day, some doing their laundry, others just idling about or cracking their books in the quiet of spring break. Most of the student body was, fortunately, someplace else. Out on a country road all alone, the Schneider family was taking a Sunday drive as the sun began setting — just mom, dad and 6-year old Darren, who were going to go bowling later, according to the *Pioneer Press*. From all reports in the Twin Cities two daily papers, the *Star Tribune*, *Pioneer Press* and an emotional collection of personal stories called *Twist of Fate* (published by the St. Peter's Kiwanis), an ordinary Minnesota Sunday in southern Minnesota was about to be severely altered, the landscape forever changed along with the lives of area residents.

At least 14 tornadoes were reported that stormy afternoon. A couple of them — spawned by a super cell that subsequently produced the F4 twister that almost leveled the farming community of Comfrey and the F3 spinner that annihilated St. Peter — were so extreme and oddly formed that experts and common folks had a hard time realizing just what they were.

"I saw it [the approaching tornado] over the top of the Nicollet Hotel building," recalls Ken Forkey in the Kiwanis' book. "A blue-black wall cloud so wide that no actual funnel was visible, but the rotation of this cloud and debris was frighteningly close." In the same publication, then-mayor of St. Pete, Jerry Hawbaker, said (before dashing into the closet of their home with his wife), "I couldn't see a funnel, but could see movement within the cloud, perhaps 200 to 400 feet high."

One year after the disasters, National Weather Service scientist Rich Naistat told Jim Dawson of the *Star Tribune* that the super cell was really a monster wedge. "We weren't aware it was a monster wedge at the time," he said. "We later found out it was one and one-fourth miles wide." Weather Service storm expert Todd Krause confirmed that perception in the same newspaper account: "This tornado was so large that there weren't many videos taken of it because people didn't recognize it as a tornado. Many people say it looked like a big fog bank coming at them."

One person from St. Peter in the Kiwanis' book reported that, "Our tornado didn't spin vertically, it spun horizontally. It was the worst thing that had happened to this town in 147 years." Dawson's newspaper account of the how the superstorm formed and unloaded its destruction in that retrospective story called, "The making of a monster," is so insightful and dramatic that readers should seek it out in its entirety. Dawson writes:

"By sundown, 14 tornadoes would hit southern Minnesota. One of them, with a funnel 1 1/4 miles wide and winds as high as 260 mph, would stay on the ground for a remarkable 67 miles; that's the tornado that almost leveled the farming town of Comfrey. Another powerful tornado that was more than a mile wide ripped apart St. Peter and everything else in its 18-mile path." When it was over the amount of damage was at first almost as incomprehensible as the few number of fatalities — only two — including little Darren Schneider.

According to the National Weather Service, the Schneider's van was blown about 100 yards off the road. It bounced around like a toy several times. His parents survived even though they were sucked out of the van with their son. The storm threw them in three different directions, as Nick Coleman vividly writes in a *Pioneer Press* interview with the Schneider's a year later. Poor little Darren was hurled 150 yards away into the mud and died.

If this tragedy had a human face, it was Darren's, and the photos, videotape and personal accounts one heard after the storm were worth thousands of words. The *Pioneer Press* reported that, "The storms were so powerful that debris from St. Peter was found Monday in Hudson, Wis., a distance of 78 miles." And in one of those anecdotes often associated with the weird and almost magical power of tornadoes, this strange one emerged from the *Twist of Fate* collection: "After the storm died own, a lady went back to where her house used to be and started looking for whatever she could salvage. She found two bottles of wine. They weren't broken and the corks were in place, but the bottles were empty!"

The statistics reported in the *Star Tribune* and told a much grimmer tale:

→ **The tornado leveled 200 homes in St. Peter, damaged more than half of the town's 3,000 houses and damaged 3,200 buildings.**

→ **It destroyed almost 2,000 trees on the Gustavus Adolphus campus and wreaked havoc on many of the old buildings that give the city character, blowing out more than 80,000 windows and toppling the steeple on the hallowed landmark of Christ Chapel.**

→ **In the heaviest-hit area near Gorman Park, two old public schools and a Catholic church complex were damaged beyond repair. The 1890s school, a mansard-roofed French style building, had just been renovated as an art center.**

→ **All told, the damage was estimated at between $300 million and $500 million.**

→ **The St. Paul Cos., a major insurance company based in the Twin Cities, posted a $175 million loss in the third quarter of 1998 — mostly because of payouts from storm damages including the southern Minnesota tornadoes.**

The *Pioneer Press* reported in the wake of the disaster and other storms less severe in 1998 that "Minnesota property owners and casualty insurers are incurring an extraordinary storm damage toll that appears sure to pass $1 billion before the last roof is repaired and windshield replaced. Insured catastrophe losses are running so high in 1998 that they surpass the combined losses chalked up in the last 31 years, says the Insurance Federation of Minnesota."

But the huge twisters that ripped through St. Peter and tore up communities like Comfrey and the surrounding farmlands on March 29, 1998, weren't supposed to happen. Not according to the weather statistics and prevailing wisdom of the area. Over 50 years, until that black Sunday, the National Weather Service only recorded four tornadoes in March, according to the *Star Tribune*. At that time of year, in fact, there is often still snow on the ground and a true nip of winter lingering in the air. As for one tornado — let alone several — blowing furiously through the region, the chances seemed slim to none: The area is set in the beautiful Minnesota River Valley, and tornadoes seldom traverse such low-lying territory. A March blizzard, yes! But violent tornados — at that time of year — in those locations? It was unthinkable.

Today the science about this specific storm has been done, although tornado science itself is far from complete. El Nino that year may have contributed to the unusually fierce weather. But maybe not. Others blamed global warming: "Maybe the planet was balking at the treatment it had been getting," said May Norton in *Twist of Fate*." Maybe. But one thing is certain, this storm created the kind of good will and fast response that few communities in the nation have ever witnessed after a natural disaster of this scope.

The call to rebuild St. Peter went out and was widely

heeded. People came from all over the region to help with medical, housing, safety and other issues — including eventually architecture and engineering experts concerned about maintaining the town's historic integrity. According to one local couple, within three days, 65 percent of the debris was removed. Neighboring colleges opened their doors to students returning from spring break. The state legislature, still doing its work at the real capitol in St. Paul, quickly financed a sizeable budget to rebuild the historic town, including a $1.35 million emergency grant for historically correct renovation that Gov. Arne Carlson signed.

The effort paid off. Today, while the painful memories linger in both the town and surrounding countryside, the restoration of the historic character of St. Peter has largely succeeded, especially among the commercial and public buildings that had to be rebuilt or repaired. According the *Star Tribune* story of May 7, 2003: "In a measure of the quality of restoration work, the town's commercial district became a National Register historic district after the tornado." There really was an indelible upside to this early seasonal outbreak of extreme tornadoes. As one resident told the Kiwanis' project, "Every cloud, even a super cell, does indeed have a silver lining."

Assistance came from far and wide to rebuild and preserve historic St. Peter.
(photo: courtesy of Eric Foss)

On March 29, 1998, a tornado that was more than a mile wide ripped through the historic town of St. Peter. (photo: Star Tribune)

The tornado leveled 200 homes in St. Peter, damaged more than half of the town's 3,000 houses and damaged 3,200 buildings. (photo: courtesy of Eric Foss)

The Boundary Waters Blowdown
July 4, 1999

It was hot and muggy the early afternoon of July 4, 1999 —
familiar Fourth of July weather that prompts Minnesotans to
head to the beach or crack open a beer in the backyard. So, as
they do every year, suburbanites fired up grills and set up chairs
on freshly mown lawns. Boaters packed coolers and cast off
onto area lakes. From Austin to Zimmerman, families headed
to Main Street to watch the annual parade.

But "up north," it was a much different picture that
year. In northeastern Minnesota, the winds blew in a change
that would impact our wilderness for generations.

On the last Independence Day of the century, a devastating windstorm ripped through the Superior National Forest,
in just 20 minutes blowing down or snapping off 40 million
trees, an estimated 25 million in Minnesota's cherished
Boundary Waters Canoe Area Wilderness. Winds of 80 to 100
miles per hour topped out at 130 miles per hour in the BWCA,
tearing a path of over 600 square miles in the Superior
National Forest, flattening trees valued at up to $18 million.

A "derecho" had hit. Spanish for "direct" or "straight
ahead," a direcho is a large, destructive windstorm, and this
was the worst Minnesota had ever seen.

With winds that strong, most Minnesotans would head
below ground, taking shelter in basements. But visitors in the
Boundary Waters had no such protection.

"Campers were capsized, hurled through the air,

A section of trees downed by weekend storms can be seen in this aerial photo taken
near Birch Lake along the Gunflint Trail in northern Minnesota Wednesday, July 6, 1999.
Helicopters and planes swooped over the Boundary Waters Canoe Area in
search of people injured or stranded by high winds and heavy rains that hit much of
northeastern Minnesota. (photo: AP)

crushed under the trees and pinned under their canoes," according to *Our Wounded Wilderness*, a book about the Boundary Waters storm by Jim Cordes. "Forest Service aircraft were kept busy evacuating the badly injured. Other victims were brought out by canoe or motorboat, then by helicopter or ambulance (once roads were cleared) to hospitals in Ely, Grand Marais, Two Harbors and others in the area. Many people were within inches of death as trees fell on them, their tents, canoes, cars, camper trailers and cabins."

The heaviest damage occurred in a path 4 to 12 miles wide and 35 miles long in the BWCA. Hundreds of campsites and portages were hit, and hundreds of rescue workers and volunteers evacuated campers from the area. In all, 60 people were injured, many airlifted out of BWCA. Miraculously, no one was killed. But with an estimated 2,500 campers in the wilderness that day, there were hundreds of near misses.

"Before we could fasten our rain gear the first blast of the storm hit us," said camper Richard Hill in *Our Wounded Wilderness*. "It was exactly 12:50. I remember looking at my watch. We couldn't believe what was happening. The blast of wind and rain uprooted and sheared off all the weaker trees on the island; they were flying in every direction and we had nowhere to go for protection. We were dodging falling trees when a group of jack pine fell on us, knocking us to the ground. Luckily, we weren't injured. We quickly dove under a group of crisscrossed jack pine and hung onto one another while the wind roared."

But it wasn't over. The rains that came the next day were the worst in memory, washing out roads, causing flooding and hampering rescue efforts. Eighty to 100 miles of power lines and nearly 250 poles were laid on the ground along the Gunflint Trail, shutting off power to 600 customers. Arrowhead Coop., which was equipped to handle replacing two to seven poles a year, was faced with suddenly replacing hundreds over the worst terrain imaginable. Arrowhead workers, aided by 70 to 80 workers from throughout the state, worked up to 16 hours daily restoring the power. It took four weeks to completely restore power to the entire system. Local churches fed the workers and washed their laundry. Gunflint Lodge provided meals for a week. Trail Center made 1,560 sandwiches. Johnson's Big Dollar provided food and water. Motels and resorts made room for the crew.

On Lake Superior, no boaters were hurt, but the lake will be affected for centuries. "Anyone driving along the North Shore of Superior July 5 saw the bruise left by the storm in the sediment stain reaching far into the lake," according to a story in the *Cook County News-Herald*. Soil and Water Conservation District Manager Rebecca Wiinanen says it will take centuries for the lake to recharge: "the same amount of time it will take for a white pine seedling planted this year to reach the height of ones felled July 4, 1999."

In a windstorm that began in North Dakota and ended in New England, even Canada was impacted, with a blowdown of 150,000 acres. Also hard-hit was Moose Lake, home of acclaimed *National Geographic* photographer Jim Brandenburg. On July 8 that year on Minnesota Public Radio, he described the impact on his world:

"It's a loss. It's a great loss that does feel like we've lost some sort of family member. There's a kind of mourning. Knowing it's a natural process helps a little bit. All death and birth is, of course, natural, but this one is on a gargantuan and very humbling scale that I have never seen in my own personal life."

Then came the politicians: Sen. Rod Grams on July 8. Cong. Jim Oberstar July 11. Gov. Jesse Ventura July 12. Sen. Paul Wellstone July 24. Soon, Pres. Clinton declared eight Minnesota counties a disaster area — Aitkin, Cass, Clay, Cook, Hubbard, Itasca, Lake and St. Louis — freeing up millions for disaster aid.

As cleanup began, worries turned to fire. The massive amount of downed timber provided kindling for wildfires, as felled trees lay across the forest floor, in some areas stacked 10 feet high. The U.S. Forest Service began a seven-year project to reduce the fuel load with controlled burning. "We're going to be living with a considerable change in the fire system up there for at least the next 10 to 20 years," said Paul Tine, fuel and fire specialist for the U.S. Forest Service, in an interview with *Cook County News-Herald.*

In the months and even years after the blowdown, some BWCA businesses were disgusted with negative reporting of the July 4 events, which they believe exaggerated the destruction and severely impacted their businesses:

"According to newspapers and television reports, the Boundary Waters Canoe Area Wilderness had been wiped off the map that day," states a 2004 newsletter from Willams & Hall Wilderness Guides & Outfitters. "These reports caused panic and confusion among visitors who had upcoming trips.

Still today, there are those who believe the news reports and refuse to visit the Boundary Waters, because they still believe that 'after all what is left to visit anyway?' Yes, there is damage ... but there are plenty of reasons remaining to visit the area. Quite possibly, even more reasons than 'pre-blowdown' because of the renewal process occurring in the storm damaged areas."

Forest officials learned from the July 4 blowdown and say they are better prepared for the next big event.

"One of the big criticisms from the 9/11 Commission was that the police and fire departments in New York never had a unified response," Cook Country Sheriff Dave Wirt told the *Minneapolis Star Tribune* in 2004. "That was us before July 4, 1999 ... But we have that unified command now. We're still meeting regularly. I think some good has come from that storm."

The forest has rebounded, and signs of renewal are everywhere. But it's a forest in transition. Jim Sanders, supervisor of the Superior National Forest, told the *Star Tribune* that the blowdown provided the opportunity to study a natural succession that otherwise would have taken decades.

"Mother Nature is so much more resilient than we humans give her credit for," said Sanders. "The ecological restoration began right after the blowdown. Northeastern Minnesota is a disturbance-based ecological system. It's either wind, insects, disease or fire, or some combination thereof, which have continuously given us the forest we have. There will be plant and wildlife species that will benefit because of it, and there will be those species that will not benefit. ... The silver lining is that no one was killed when Mother Nature did this disturbance. And now we have the opportunity to learn from a landscape-scale event how change takes place."

Indeed, eight years after the blowdown, perspective is key. "Some may view the act of Mother Nature as utter devastation. Others, however, may look in wonder as they chart the changes and growth of a new and healthier forest emerging literally from the ashes of the storm," states the Willams & Hall Outfitters newsletter.

Although the forest is changing, there are some things that are certain, say the outfitters: "The fish still bite, the loon still share their enchanting call, and the eagles still soar in the air currents. Nature, and the wilderness it lives within, continues on in spite of the straight-line winds of July 4, 1999."

Eighty to 100 miles of power lines and nearly 250 poles were laid on the ground along the Gunflint Trail, shutting off power to 600 customers. (photo: Star Tribune)

On the last Independence Day of the century, a devastating windstorm ripped through the Superior National Forest, in just 20 minutes blowing down or snapping off 40 million trees like toothpicks, an estimated 25 million in Minnesota's cherished Boundary Waters Canoe Area Wilderness. (photo: Star Tribune)

One lone house stands amid the devastation of the Boundary Waters Blowdown,
July 1999. (photo: AP/The Duluth News-Tribune, Renee Knoeber)

COMING UP

More Storms Brewing ...

Did we miss your most memorable Minnesota storm in this book? Don't worry — we're not done yet! Watch for another *Storms!* book coming up, with major weather events including:

→ **The 1965 Tornadoes** that roared through Minnesota, devastating Fridley and earning fame as the greatest weather disaster in Twin Cities history.

→ **The 1930s Dust Bowl**, ranked #1 on the Minnesota Climatology Office list of Top Weather Events of the 20th Century.

→ **The 1997 Red River Flood**, peaking at East Grand Forks more than 26 feet above flood stage, causing damage in Minnesota alone in the hundreds of millions of dollars.

Stay tuned for this book! But first, see what's next in the Minnesota Series:

Minnesota Music

Bob Dylan

In our very next book in the Minnesota Series, former pop music writer Martin Keller will look at the Minnesota music scene from the late '50s to the '80s – right before the Purple Reign of Prince, the flight of The Jayhawks, Jonny Lang and a host of other homegrown music makers. Track your favorite period in Minnesota's rich music culture, from Big Reggie's Danceland to "Funkytown," from the innocent guitar twang of the Soma Records '60s to the new wave assault of Twin/Tone Records.

Don't miss this jam-packed jukebox flashback!